THE JOYFUL STOIC JOURNAL

This Journal belongs to

_____

Copyright © 2019 Bien Inc

All Rights Reserved

ISBN: 978-0-578-22154-0

THE JOYFUL STOIC;

A brief introduction to Stoicism and weekly journal

In memory of my Mother Christie, and
Father William for nurturing my curiosity

Table of Contents

1. Forward	13
2. Introduction- Why You Need Philosophy	15
Part I	
3. Sages	22
4. The Basics of Stoicism	23
5. Stoic Goals	23
Part II	
6. Control	30
7. Gratitude	44
8. Negative Visualization	46
9. Ephemeralism	50
10. Immunity from Life's Pleasures and Pain	55
11. Detachment from Wealth	78
12. Duty & Social Relationships	90
13. External Influences	95
14. Focus on The Present	105
15. Meditations	113
16. Life Goals	122
Notes & Acknowledgments	124

Foreword

If I recall correctly, I met Amas more than 15 years ago. Although our connection was through business, it always seemed like much more - perhaps one of those distant friendships where you start conversations months -or years later- where you left off. Then sev-eral years ago we began to talk about working together. We talked many times about life values and personal perspectives - on faith and family and life. And now we find ourselves working with clients and speaking on stage together.

Much like my recent path, this book talks about his path to make sense of life.

My wife and I experienced the worse kind of pain almost two years ago when our thirty-four year-old daughter died of meta-static breast cancer. Her amazing four-year survivor fight helped us understand even more deeply that a "life well lived"is really about inward growth and relationships. Who you are at your core allows you to survive the worse and celebrate even better. Whether through a path of faith or just through realization that family and friendships - are the catalyst of success and happiness. We called her the Warrior Princess and her motto during her fight became, "Be silly. Be brave. Be kind." It was a life well lived - although far too short.

I love how in this book, Amas explores his personal journey and then provides a "journal" for discovery. His writing is true to his spirit - creative, consistent, focused. But it also confirms the fun times we have had - first as distant friends and more recently as "family" - perhaps as a "big brother" (with both of us playing that role depending on the situation). There have been deep philosophical discussion over vodka martinis and sugar-rimmed lemon drops (his cocktail of choice).

I hope that your new journey begins inside these pages. That you will follow Amas as he helps you find joy....

Joy within yourself.

- Bob Furniss.

Bob is an internationally renowned Contact Center Consultant and was recently presented with the lifetime achievement award by ICMI.

Why You need Philosophy

I am no different than most, I have a moral compass, I was raised in a christian household and today I spend most of my time trying to lead a better and better life. Until a couple years ago the best way to describe myself would be what william Irvine calls an "Enlightened Hedonist". Frankly it is the default guiding philosophy for most of us in the west. We chase affluence, status, have some moral compass and chase increasing pleasures.

My quest to make sure my life had a guiding philosophy was not a theoretical exercise it was a practical one. I want to make sure I don't waste my life pursuing the wrong things. Remember I said like most people I had wrongly focused on living a better, more pleasurable life. In a practical sense, let's take a look at a basic question I asked myself and you should ask yourself too. How much money do I want to make? I spend a lot of time making a living so understanding what the destination is should be known. You should ask yourself the same question. Exactly how much money do you want to make? I suspect that your answer is some variant of the word - 'MORE'. I used to proudly say that the answer is always "More". If you like me think deep down that answer is inherently flawed then keep reading.

Are you familiar with the Hedonic treadmill? You can look further into it, but the basic premise is that as you acquire what you want - let's say money, you get a temporary bump in happiness, you get used to that level of wealth, then the happiness bump goes away and you therefore need even more wealth. So trying to live a better life as defined by more wealth and pleasures can not be it. I needed a life philosophy and I think you do too.

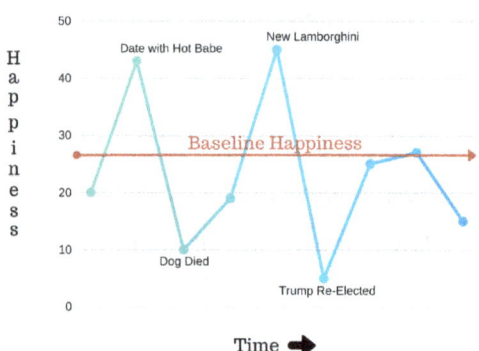

If the Hedonistic Treadmill is a bad idea, then what is better? I dabbled in different philosophies of life over the years, most of them were disqualified in my mind for a number of reasons. Bluntly some of them required too much effort, and like a strict diet it won't stick with me. For me the right philosophy shouldn't set me up for failure. I for example, have no desire to go spend my days as a Buddhist Monk. Many other philosophies didn't engage me intellectually enough, some I flat out just disagreed with.

I want to persuade you that separate and apart from your belief and faith or lack thereof, your life needs a guiding philosophy, you can pick one, or take ideas from several.

Four years ago I found a 2,000 year old philosophy called Stoicism, and it has been the most pleasantly surprising journey of enlightenment so far. If you think of Stoicism, the first mistake you might make is to confuse (lowercase) stoicism with (uppercase) Stoicism. I too thought of Stoics same way you probably do, unfeeling, robotic, lack of joy. Let me assure you the Stoics were none of those things - it represents the opposite.

One other thing I want to get out of the way is religion and faith. The following pages are not about what happens after we die, or about your faith or religion. It is more about arming you with tools rooted in ancient philosophy and psychology that will bring you Stoic Joy.

Other authors have done a good job going deep into the history and documenting the odds and ins of Stoicism, I plan to do two things, expose you to Stoicism, and then provide you with a journal that will help you practice its counsel.

PART I
A Brief Introduction to Stoicism

Life Goals

Do you have a life goal? Not the things you want in life through the years but your overarching life goal. If you do, write it here. If you have not given this much thought before that is fine, you are not alone, we will come back to this.

Day_____Date: __/__/__

My grand goal for life is to

_____

_____

_____

_____

_____

_____

_____

_____

Do you have a life strategy (Philosophy)?

Assuming you have clarity on life's grand goals, do you have a strategy to get you there. Less important things like your finances often require hiring a financial advisor or at least having a financial plan.

The reason you do that is to make sure you don't waste your valuable financial resources. For your grand goal in life you should have some insurance to make sure you do not waste your life on pursuits not worth chasing.

What about Faith?

If you are reading this and thinking you are a person of faith and therefore do not need a life philosophy. Allow me to challenge that thinking. Suppose you are a Christian, your pastor or priest is concerned about you living a morally upright life that includes prayer, tithing or all the things that allow you to make it in heaven - in other words the concern is your soul. What is not of your pastor's concern is what you should pursue in life - you can choose to spend your life chasing wealth, live in a big mansion, so long as you don't break any laws. You can also live your life in a one bedroom apartment in the worst neighborhoods if you choose. My point is most religions and faiths don't require you to have a life philosophy so long as you live a morally upright life and follow it's traditions.

I am not here to ask you to join a formal school of philosophy but to invite you to add more arrows in your quiver on the journey of life.

The Stoic Sages

There have been many prominent stoics over the years but the three who did the best job of articulating what being a stoic is all about - Marcus Aurelius, Seneca, and Epictetus.

While there is not a Stoic Manual, the writings of the three principals are required reading - Marcus Arellius who was the Roman Empire journaled his thoughts about humility, life meaning and compassion. Epictetus whose work is less accessible was born a slave and ended up teaching Stoic Philosophy in Rome. Lastly, Seneca the most accessible of the three. I read Seneca almost every single day, he wrote letters to mentees addressing every day issues, from grief, anger, grief and much more. Even though his work is 2,000 years old the advice is still very practical today. I am introducing these Sages now as their words will be a recurring theme in the following pages.

If you can only buy one book, but letters from a Stoic by Seneca. I read something from it almost daily.

Stoicism Basics

Stoicism is a 2,000+ year old philosophy that began about 300 years B.C that is focused on pursuing two grand goals - Tranquility and Stoic virtue. There are specific practices that will help you achieve the tranquility we are referring to here, not a Xanax fueled emotionless state. But tranquility that is instead marked by the absence of things like fear, anxiety, grief and the presence of Joy. Mastering these negative emotions and perceptions does not mean you do not feel them, it means you are in control. It is a school of thought that takes from older philosophies and injects plenty of psychological techniques to help its adherent constantly strive for perfecting the Stoic sage goal.

For me it is the aspirational goal of achieving Stoic joy whether I am wealthy, poor or experiencing other life's discomforts. None of these things will impact my disposition, and while there is no perfect Sage, the implementation of practices will help me get closer to this goal.

Stoic Grand Goal

One thing that this philosophy makes very clear is what you should not pursue - Fame and Fortune. I would say those are the worst grand goals in order of which is worse for you. Pursuit of

Fame and fortune will not bring you tranquility. While stoics do not advocate chasing wealth, it's view of wealth can be summed up in this quote.

"We should acquire an amount that does not descend to poverty and yet is not far removed from poverty" - Seneca

The stoics also saw danger in the luxuries of life, and espoused taking joy in enjoying simple things. In other words our basic human needs are very basic and while we may have resources, we should have an indifference to wealth. In other words, whether you are poor or rich, do not chase luxuries, enjoy simple things. Epictetus said "It is better to die of hunger with distress and fear gone than to live upset in the midst of plenty". You must not NEED your wealth is the key takeaway.

The stoics were less nuanced about fame. The sages all have one advice - RUN far away from pursuing fame - the pursuit of fame requires you to chase external validation and it is near impossible to chase fame and maintain your stoic principles.

"He who has a vehement desire for posthumous fame does not consider that every one of those who remember him will himself also die very soon." - Marcus Arellius

If you are to adopt Stoicism that means your grand goal is to practice stoic Virtue and achieve Tranquility. In this one sentence is a lot, plenty of things you must avoid and seek to ensure success on this journey.

Tranquility & Virtue

Tranquility is not living like a zombie, unable to feel and motionless, but it is the absence of negative emotions and the presence of stoic Joy. How you achieve this requires some effort, especially if like me you don't plan on moving to a Buddhist monk. The good news is the Stoics used a lot of practices rooted in philosophy and psychology to help you achieve this, in the coming pages I plan to help you with some of the practices that have helped countless others along the way.

Virtue in the stoic sense is not for all of us to take the abstinence pledge and go into the priesthood, it is instead a call to live in accordance with nature. That virtue is based on using our brains to chase the right things to spend your life on. Living the virtuous life will bring you tranquility. Think of tranquility as the byproduct of living in stoic virtue.

Lastly, this is not an invitation to join a cult, a religion or a sect, but for you to take the principles of this philosophy and apply them into your life. It will require some effort and change, but I trust that you will find that while it is not as difficult as becoming a Buddhist monk the effort required will pay off and be meaningful.

The next section of this book focuses on the Stoic Tools, and ways to put them in practice.

Part II
Core Stoic Practices & Journal

Control

Similar to other philosophies, Stoicism encourages us to not expend energy on things we have no control over. Focus on things we have control - our reactions, our emotions, the goals we set. We do not control outcomes directly, or other people's behavior. So at my job or when I play sports - I can control how hard I work, how I react to things, what goals I set - but I do not obsess over the outcome. Seneca for example would not set a goal to change the world, but his goal was to instead practice and teach stoicism so that more people would lead virtuous lives.

Control

"You have power over your mind – not outside events. Realize this, and you will find strength."- Marcus Aurelius

Day_____Date: __/__/__

What outside events have taken your mind hostage and how will I prevent that today..

_____

_____

_____

_____

_____

_____

_____

_____

Control

"Just keep in mind: the more we value things outside our control, the less control we have." -Epictetus

Think about your worries in work, with family and in life, start setting the right goals. Goals centered on your actions and thoughts and not the outcomes or other people's actions.

Day_____Date: __/__/__

_____
_____
_____
_____
_____
_____
_____
_____

Control

"If you are easily provoked you are easily controlled." -Marcus Arellius

Day_____Date: __/__/__

I can't control the actions of others, only my reaction....

_____

_____

_____

_____

_____

_____

_____

_____

_____

Control

"I will not be controlled by fear of shame or ridicule."-Amas Tenumah

Day_____Date: __/__/__

_____

_____

_____

_____

_____

_____

_____

_____

_____

Control

"The chief task in life is simply this: to identify and separate matters so that I can say clearly to myself which are externals not under my control, and which have to do with the choices I actually control. Where then do I look for good and evil? Not to uncontrollable externals, but within myself to the choices that are my own." -Epictetus

Day_____Date: __/__/__

I can't control the actions of others, only my reaction....

_____

_____

_____

_____

_____

_____

_____

Control

"I'm not going to let these external things disturb me" - Seneca

Day_____Date: __/__/__

I can't control the actions of others, only my reaction....

_____

_____

_____

_____

_____

_____

_____

_____

_____

_____

Control

"Make the best use of what is in your power, and take the rest as it happens. Some things are up to us and some things are not up to us." – Epictetus

Day_____Date: __/__/__

I can't control the actions of others, only my reaction....

_____

_____

_____

_____

_____

_____

_____

Control

"Man conquers the world by conquering himself." -Zeno of Citium

Day_____Date: __/__/__

Conquering myself is about being in control of my own perceptions...

_____

_____

_____

_____

_____

_____

_____

_____

Control

"Today I escaped anxiety. Or no, I discarded it, because it was within me, in my own perceptions – not outside." -Marcus Aurelius

Day_____Date: __/__/__

_____

_____

_____

_____

_____

_____

_____

_____

_____

Control

"Learn to be indifferent to what makes no difference." -Marcus Aurelius

Day_____Date: __/__/__

The list of what makes no difference includes opinions of everyone about you...

_____

_____

_____

_____

_____

_____

_____

_____

_____

Control

"What upsets people is not things themselves, but their judgements about these things." -Epictetus

Day_____Date: __/__/__

Control

"Why is this so unbearable? Why can't I endure it? You'll be embarrassed to answer." -Marcus Aurelius

Day_____Date: __/__/__

_____

_____

_____

_____

_____

_____

_____

_____

_____

_____

Control

"You have power over your mind — not outside events. Realize this, and you will find strength." -Marcus Aurelius

Day_____Date: __/__/__

_____

_____

_____

_____

_____

_____

_____

_____

_____

_____

Gratitude

"A man thus grounded must, whether he wills or not, necessarily be attended by constant cheerfulness and a joy that is deep and issues from deep within, since he finds delight in his own resources, and desires no joys greater than his inner joys." -Seneca

Day_____Date: __/__/__

_____

_____

_____

_____

_____

_____

_____

_____

Negative Visualization
(premeditatio malorum)

Similar to being thankful, the stoics advocate contemplating loss periodically (maybe a couple times a week to start). In practice it goes like this. You imagine losing the people or things most meaningful to you with two goals in mind. The stoics teach us that the goal is twofold. One is to appreciate the people in your life and therefore not take them for granted, and secondly be prepared for loss. When I practice this in my own life, at times I look at my son and I contemplate losing him as painful as the thought is - I get more grateful for my time with him and I am more present.

Negative Visualization (premeditatio malorum)

Close your eyes and imagine losing something that is important to you. Write down your thoughts below, the focus on the pain, but also on your sense of gratitude.

Day_____Date: __/__/__

'Remember that all we have is "on loan" from Fortune, which can reclaim it without our permission – indeed, without even advance notice" - Seneca

_____

_____

_____

_____

_____

_____

_____

_____

Negative Visualization

Close your eyes and imagine losing someone that is important to you. Write down your thoughts below, the focus on the pain, but also on your sense of gratitude.

'Remember that all we have is "on loan" from Fortune, which can reclaim it without our permission – indeed, without even advance notice. Thus, we should love all our dear ones, but always with the thought that we have no promise that we may keep them forever – nay, no promise even that we may keep them for long.'– Seneca

Day_____Date: __/__/__

_____

_____

_____

_____

_____

_____

_____

Ephemeralism

"Life is short, and we are a very small part of what has come and what will come. So all we have is to take advantage of NOW. Alexander the Great and his mule driver both died and the same thing happened to both." – Marcus Aurelius

Day_____Date: __/__/__

_____

_____

_____

_____

_____

_____

_____

_____

_____

Ephemeralism

"The worry is now how you will be remembered, it is how did you really live in private, away from scrutiny." - Amas Tenumah

Day_____Date: __/__/__

_____

_____

_____

_____

_____

_____

_____

_____

_____

Ephemeralism

"Run down the list of those who felt intense anger at something: the most famous, the most unfortunate, the most hated, the most whatever: Where is all that now? Smoke, dust, legend...or not even a legend. Think of all the examples. And how trivial the things we want so passionately are." -Marcus Aurelius

Day_____Date: __/__/__

_____

_____

_____

_____

_____

_____

_____

Ephemeralism

"Chasing legacy is not worthwile, everyone who will ever remember will be dead and gone." -Amas Tenumah

Day_____Date: __/__/__

_____

_____

_____

_____

_____

_____

_____

_____

_____

_____

Immunity to Life's Hardships & Pleasures

Your worth and joy should not be tied to your material comforts. We are encouraged to have an inner joy that is driven from within. So strong that if you lost your home you will be just as thankful as one who lives in a mansion.

One of my favorite parts of Stoicism is it's hands on nature. The sages espoused this idea that we should be indifferent to life's comforts. In other words my disposition should not be disrupted because I am rich, or poor. So building on the practice of negative visualization - The Stoics take it to a whole new level. If the premise is that my comforts no matter how small or large do not impact my Joy. So we should practice actual hardship, I do this regularly. In my case the benefits have been enormous, I take cold showers on cold days, spend nights in a shelter, and I can go on. Truth is I am scared to death of some discomforts and I get two benefits from practicing the discomforts.

1.) I am confident that no matter what my fortunes I will be fine and will maintain my tranquility and gratitude.
2.) I am more thankful and grateful because I practice hardships.

More Immunity Exercises

Now your turn, write down how you will harden yourself today

_____

_____

_____

_____

_____

_____

_____

_____

_____

_____

_____

Now your turn, write down how you will harden yourself today. For inspiration, I took a cold shower today. Write about your experience, what did you learn.

Today I woke up in a homeless shelter. I was not stoic about the experience. Do something today to harden your immunity to comfort, write and grow. You can start small.

"But there is no bitterness in doing without that which you have ceased to desire." - Seneca

Now your turn, write down how you will harden yourself this week, write what was hard and understand why.

_____

_____

_____

_____

_____

_____

_____

_____

_____

Think about the things you enjoy the most - this week do without it. For me it was great food, I would fast and when I eat it was only oatmeal, I despise oatmeal, I can now live on oatmeal

Now your turn, write down how you will harden yourself this week, write what was hard and understand why.

_____

_____

_____

_____

_____

_____

_____

_____

_____

"How ridiculous and how strange to be surprised at anything which happens in life." - *Marcus Aurelius*

This is an aspirational quote - imperviousness to hardships or pleasures. Now your turn, write down how you will harden yourself this week, write what was hard and understand why.

_____

_____

_____

_____

_____

_____

_____

_____

_____

Count all the times you were not grateful because of minor inconveniences, I regret my reaction every time, but you put yourself in those circumstances, so it hardens your spine.

Now your turn, write down how you will harden yourself this week, write what was hard and understand why.

_____

_____

_____

_____

_____

_____

_____

_____

_____

I wore mismatched, torn clothing out today, I was humiliated, I wrote about why clothes that keep me warm aren't good enough.

Now your turn, write down how you will harden yourself this week, write what was hard and understand why.

_____

_____

_____

_____

_____

_____

_____

_____

I stayed at the four seasons on a work trip and spent the following night at a motel 6 and journaled on my feelings bout both, the goal is I should be impervious to either end.

Now your turn, write down how you will harden yourself this week, write what was hard and understand why.

_____

_____

_____

_____

_____

_____

_____

_____

_____

Are you noticing the delta in your feelings when experiencing pleasure and pain? What accounts for it?

Now your turn, write down how you will harden yourself this week, write what was hard and understand why.

_____

_____

_____

_____

_____

_____

_____

_____

I hope you are getting better and more immune, keep journaling.

Now your turn, write down how you will harden yourself this week, write what was hard and understand why.

_____

_____

_____

_____

_____

_____

_____

_____

_____

_____

I drank only water for three days.

Now your turn, write down how you will harden yourself this week, write what was hard and understand why.

_____

_____

_____

_____

_____

_____

_____

_____

_____

I went to a party and didn't drink at all.

Now your turn, write down how you will harden yourself this week, write what was hard and understand why.

_____

_____

_____

_____

_____

_____

_____

_____

_____

I ran in the freezing cold today.

Now your turn, write down how you will harden yourself this week, write what was hard and understand why.

_____

_____

_____

_____

_____

_____

_____

_____

_____

I skipped ESPN for a month.

Now your turn, write down how you will harden yourself this week, write what was hard and understand why.

_____

_____

_____

_____

_____

_____

_____

_____

_____

I spent 2 days without WiFi.

Now your turn, write down how you will harden yourself this week, write what was hard and understand why.

_____

_____

_____

_____

_____

_____

_____

_____

_____

I fasted for two days.

Now your turn, write down how you will harden yourself this week, write what was hard and understand why.

_____

_____

_____

_____

_____

_____

_____

_____

_____

I walked for 16 miles with my car in the garage.

Now your turn, write down how you will harden yourself this week, write what was hard and understand why.

_____

_____

_____

_____

_____

_____

_____

_____

_____

I love my bed, I spent the night under a bridge.

Now your turn, write down how you will harden yourself this week, write what was hard and understand why.

_____

_____

_____

_____

_____

_____

_____

_____

_____

Document your progress and failures.

Now your turn, write down how you will harden yourself this week, write what was hard and understand why.

_____

_____

_____

_____

_____

_____

_____

_____

_____

Detachment from Wealth

"Your food should appease your hunger, your drink quench your thirst, your clothing keep out the cold, your house be a protection against inclement weather. It makes no difference whether it is built of turf or of variegated marble imported from another country." - Seneca

Day_____Date: __/__/__

_____

_____

_____

_____

_____

_____

_____

_____

Detachment from Wealth

"Set aside now and then a number of days during which you will be content with the plainest of food, and very little of it, and with rough, coarse clothing, and will ask yourself, 'Is this what one used to dread?" -Seneca

Day_____Date: __/__/__

_____

_____

_____

_____

_____

_____

_____

_____

_____

Detachment from Wealth

"He who has made a fair compact with poverty is Rich." - Seneca

Day_____Date: __/__/__

Detachment from Wealth

No good thing renders its possesor happy, unless his mind is reconciled to the possibility of loss; nothing, however, is lost with less discomfort that that which, when lost, cannot be missed.

Day_____Date: __/__/__

_____

_____

_____

_____

_____

_____

_____

_____

Detachment from Wealth

"Philosophy calls for plain living, but not for penance; and we may perfectly well be plain and neat at the same time." - Seneca

Day_____ Date: __/__/__

_____

_____

_____

_____

_____

_____

_____

_____

_____

_____

Detachment from Wealth

"It is not the man who has too little, but the man who craves more, that is poor." -Seneca

Day_____Date: __/__/__

_____

_____

_____

_____

_____

_____

_____

_____

_____

_____

_____

Detachment from Wealth

"Wealth consists not in having great possessions, but in having few wants." -Epictetus

Day_____Date: __/__/__

_____

_____

_____

_____

_____

_____

_____

_____

_____

_____

Detachment from Wealth

*"Never have I put my trust in fortune, even when she appeared to be offering peace; all those gifts she bestowed on me in her kindness — **money**, position, influence — I stored where she would be able to reclaim them with no disturbance to me."* -Seneca

Day_____Date: __/__/__

Detachment from Wealth

"The wise man is neither raised up by prosperity nor cast down by adversity; for always he has striven to rely predominantly on himself, and to derive all joy from himself." -Seneca

Day_____Date: __/__/__

Detachment from Wealth

"If you lose all you own today will you be less happy?" Write your honest feelings and reflect on them." - Amas Tenumah

Day_____Date: __/__/__

_____

_____

_____

_____

_____

_____

_____

_____

_____

_____

Detachment from Wealth

"In the mean time, cling tooth and nail to the following rule: not to give in to adversity, not to trust prosperity, and always take full note of fortune's habit of behaving just as she pleases." -Seneca

Day_____Date: __/__/__

_____

_____

_____

_____

_____

_____

_____

_____

Duty & Social Relations

There is a dilema in being Stoic and living on the face of the earth, especially in our culture of MORE. Our hedonistic culture that celebrates fame, wealth, affluence, influence and prestige. How can you keep your philosophy and not for example start chasing fame? We do it by being vigilant and putting our tools as outlined in this book to use.

"When you wake up in the morning, tell yourself: the people I deal with today will be meddling, ungrateful, arrogant, dishonest, jealous and surly. They are like this because they can't tell good from evil." -Marcus Aurelius

Day_____Date: __/__/__

_____

_____

_____

_____

_____

Duty & Social Relations

"Don't explain your philosophy. Embody it." -Epictetus

Day_____Date: __/__/__

_____

_____

_____

_____

_____

_____

_____

_____

_____

_____

_____

Duty & Social Relations

"Inwardly, we ought to be different in every respect, but our outward dress should blend in with the crowd." -Seneca

Seeking external gratification is not what this practice is all about. Your reward is the internal stoic joy.

Day_____Date: __/__/__

_____

_____

_____

_____

_____

_____

_____

_____

Duty & Social Relations

"Public shame and ridicule exerts too much control over you. You must practice so you are immune to its reign over you. I went out in public yesterday in mismatching clothes so I could build my immunity. What will you do to harden your spirit?" - Amas Tenumah

Day_____Date: __/__/__

_____

_____

_____

_____

_____

_____

_____

_____

External Influences

There are two main points about external influences, one is you obviously can't control it, and two, it is poison.

I"f you are ever tempted to look for outside approval, realize that you have compromised your integrity. If you need a witness, be your own." -Epictetus

Day_____Date: __/__/__

_____

_____

_____

_____

_____

_____

_____

_____

External Influences

"Think about all the people who will cause you to be less tranquil today, how will you handle it?" - Amas Tenumah

Day_____Date: __/__/__

_____

_____

_____

_____

_____

_____

_____

_____

_____

External Influences

"When someone is properly grounded in life, they shouldn't have to look outside themselves for approval." -Epictetus

Day_____Date: __/__/__

_____

_____

_____

_____

_____

_____

_____

_____

_____

External Influences

"You need not look about for the reward of a just deed; a just deed in itself offers a still greater return." -Seneca

This philosophy strongly beliefs that getting accolades for a good deed taints it, the entire reward is the deed itself - in private.

Day_____Date: __/__/__

_____

_____

_____

_____

_____

_____

_____

_____

External Influences

"The happiness of those who want to be popular depends on others; the happiness of those who seek pleasure fluctuates with moods outside their control; but the happiness of the wise grows out of their own free acts." -Marcus Aurelius

Day_____Date: __/__/__

_____

_____

_____

_____

_____

_____

_____

_____

_____

External Influences

"Natural desires are limited; but those which spring from false opinion have no stopping point." - Seneca

Day_____Date: __/__/__

_____

_____

_____

_____

_____

_____

_____

_____

_____

External Influences

"If anyone tells you that a certain person speaks ill of you, do not make excuses about what is said of you but answer, 'He was ignorant of my other faults, else he would not have mentioned these alone'." -Epictetus

Day_____Date: __/__/__

_____

_____

_____

_____

_____

_____

_____

_____

_____

External Influences

"Think about all the people who will cause you to be less tranquil today, how will you handle it?"- Amas Tenumah

Day_____Date: __/__/__

_____

_____

_____

_____

_____

_____

_____

_____

_____

_____

Focus on the Present

"Forget everything else. Keep hold of this alone and remember it: Each of us lives only now, this brief instant. The rest has been lived already, or is impossible to see."- Marcus Aurelius

Day_____Date: __/__/__

_____

_____

_____

_____

_____

_____

_____

_____

_____

Focus on the Present

"The present alone can make no man wretched."-Seneca

Day_____Date: __/__/__

_____

_____

_____

_____

_____

_____

_____

_____

_____

_____

Focus on the Present

"All you need are these: certainty of judgment in the present moment; action for the common good in the present moment; and an attitude of gratitude in the present moment for anything that comes your way." -Marcus Aurelius

Day_____Date: __/__/__

Focus on the Present

"My life goal is not to live a legacy, or be remembered it is to live a virtuous life today in accordance to nature." - Amas Tenumah

Day_____Date: __/__/__

_____

_____

_____

_____

_____

_____

_____

_____

_____

Focus on the Present

"Objective judgment, at this very moment. Unselfish action, now at this very moment. Willing acceptance – now at this very moment – of all external events. That's all you need." -Marcus Aurelius

Day_____Date: __/__/__

_____

_____

_____

_____

_____

_____

_____

_____

Focus on the Present

"Discard your misperceptions. Stop being jerked like a puppet. Limit yourself to the present." -Marcus Aurelius

Day_____Date: __/__/__

_____

_____

_____

_____

_____

_____

_____

_____

_____

_____

Focus on the Present

"This is the mark of perfection of character – to spend each day as if it were your last, without frenzy, laziness, or any pretending."
– Marcus Aurelius

Day_____Date: __/__/__

_____

_____

_____

_____

_____

_____

_____

_____

_____

Meditations

"If it's endurable, then endure it. Stop complaining."-Marcus Aurelius

Day_____Date: __/__/__

_____

_____

_____

_____

_____

_____

_____

_____

_____

_____

Meditations

"When you are travelling on the road, there is an end; when astray your wandering are limitless." - Seneca

Day_____Date: __/__/__

_____

_____

_____

_____

_____

_____

_____

_____

_____

Meditations

"At whatever point you have off living, provided you leave off nobly, your life is whole." - Seneca

Day_____Date: __/__/__

_____

_____

_____

_____

_____

_____

_____

_____

_____

_____

Meditations

"Waste no more time arguing about what a good man should be. Be one."- Marcus

Day_____Date: __/__/__

_____

_____

_____

_____

_____

_____

_____

_____

_____

_____

Meditations

"It can ruin your life only if it ruins your character. Otherwise it cannot harm you — inside or out." - Marcus Aurelius

Day_____Date: __/__/__

_____

_____

_____

_____

_____

_____

_____

_____

_____

Meditations

"If you seek tranquility, do less. Or (more accurately) do what's essential – what the reason of a social being requires, and in the requisite way. Which brings a double satisfaction: to do less, better." -Marcus Aurelius

Day_____Date: __/__/__

_____

_____

_____

_____

_____

_____

_____

_____

_____

Meditations

"Everything we hear is an opinion, not a fact. Everything we see is a perspective, not the truth." -Marcus Aurelius

Day_____Date: __/__/__

_____

_____

_____

_____

_____

_____

_____

_____

_____

_____

Meditations

"You are afraid of dying. But, come now, how is this life of yours anything but death?" – Seneca

Day_____Date: __/__/__

_____

_____

_____

_____

_____

_____

_____

_____

Life Goals

Let's go back to this exercise. Do you have a life goal? Not the things you want in life through the years but your overarching life goal. If you do, now write it here.

Day_____Date: __/__/__

My grand goal for life is to

_____

_____

_____

_____

_____

_____

_____

Life Goals continued...

Notes, Acknowledgments & References

1.) A Guide to the Good Life by William Irvine - The most comprehensive Introduction to stoicism

2.) Letters from a Stoic - Seneca - My daily reference guide for Philosophy

3.) The Daily Stoic https://dailystoic.com

4.) Meditations by Marcus Aurelius

5.) Discourses by Epictetus

6.) Life Hacks http://NJlifehacks.com

Without these resources this journal would not have been possible.

For More on Joyful Stoic

Please contact me if you want to discuss further, I am available on all social media platforms with the handle @amastenumah your purchase of this book also gives you access to special content on http://joyfulstoic.com

We hope you will join the movement on joyfulstoic.com

www.ingramcontent.com/pod-product-compliance
Lightning Source LLC
Chambersburg PA
CBHW071407290426
44108CB00014B/1715